wild flowers

i-SPY

INTRODUCTION

The first flowering plants appeared on Earth some 200 million years ago and since then they have spread all over the planet. Not all plants produce flowers but as flowering plants are so adaptable to different conditions, they have become the most successful type of plant around. Ultimately, all animal life depends on plants: they provide the food we eat and the air we breathe.

We depend on plants in other ways too. Many medicines were originally obtained from plants, and some still are derived from them today. The tall spikes of Foxgloves produce a drug called digitalis which is used to treat heart conditions in humans. Even aspirin was originally made from the Willow tree. So plants are not just beautiful; they are a vital part of all life on Earth.

Wild flowers grow in our gardens, parks, hedgerows, along roadsides, in and around farmland and even in rubbish dumps. Some of them grow on tiny strips of earth between pavements or through gravel driveways. You can even look out for them when you go on holiday to the seaside.

As more countryside is built upon, some wild flowers have fewer areas in which to grow, so when you go out into the countryside remember a simple rule:

'Take only photographs! Leave only footprints'. Hopefully many other people will then be able to enjoy the wild flowers you find.

How to use your i-SPY book

You will notice that the flowers in this book are arranged in groups based on their colour. You need 1000 points to send off for your i-SPY certificate (see page 64) but that is not too difficult because there are masses of points in every book. Each entry has a star or circle and points value beside it. The stars represent harder to spot entries. As you make each i-SPY, write your score in the circle or star. There are questions dotted throughout the book that can double your i-SPY score. Check your answers on page 63.

Points: 15

WOOD ANEMONE

Scientific name
Anemone nemorosa
When does it flower?
March–May
Where is it found?
Open woods and hedges
What does it look like?
About 6–30 cm (2–12 in.) tall
with a white flower sometimes
tinged pink

WHITE WATER-LILY

Points: 15

Scientific name
Nymphaea alba
When does it flower?
June–September
Where is it found?
Lakes and ponds
What does it look like?
Floating leaves with large,
decorative flowers

WILD STRAWBERRY

Points: 15 15

Scientific name
Fragaria vesca
When does it flower?
April–July
Where is it found?
Woods and shady roadsides
What does it look like?
Sprawling stems with long runners

25 **Points: 25**   Top Spot!

WOODRUFF

Scientific name
Galium odoratum
When does it flower?
April–June
Where is it found?
In woods
What does it look like?
Has bright green leaves edged with tiny prickles

This plant often grows in ancient woodland

5 Points: 5

WHITE CLOVER

Scientific name
Trifolium repens
When does it flower?
June–September
Where is it found?
Open, grassy places
What does it look like?
Low stems with three leaves

COMMON SCURVYGRASS

Points: 10

Scientific name
Cochlearia officinalis
When does it flower?
April–August
Where is it found?
Sea cliffs and along salted roadsides
What does it look like?
Lots of smooth, fleshy, heart-shaped leaves

GARLIC MUSTARD

Points: 15
Double with answer

Scientific name
Alliaria petiolata
When does it flower?
April–July
Where is it found?
Open woods and hedges
What does it look like?
Tall, hairy stems with crinkled leaves which smell of garlic when handled

Do you know any other names for this plant?

Points: 15

WILD RADISH

Scientific name
Raphanus raphanistrum
When does it flower?
May–September
Where is it found?
Farmland and waste ground
What does it look like?
Tall with flowers that can vary in colour from white to purple, and sometimes from light orange to yellow

Points: 10

WHITE CAMPION

Scientific name
Silene latifolia
When does it flower?
June–September
Where is it found?
Dry fields and roadsides
What does it look like?
Tall with sweet-scented flowers

GREATER STITCHWORT

Points: 10

Scientific name
Stellaria holostea
When does it flower?
May–June
Where is it found?
Woods and hedgerows
What does it look like?
The tall flowering stems are
four-sided and easily broken

COMMON CHICKWEED

Points: 5

Scientific name
Stellaria media
When does it flower?
Throughout the year
Where is it found?
Farms, gardens, roadsides,
seashores
What does it look like?
Sprawling and leafy with small
flowers

Points: 20

WOOD SORREL

Scientific name
Oxalis acetosella
When does it flower?
April–June
Where is it found?
Shady woods and
hedgebanks
What does it look like?
Low-growing with leaves
similar to clover

Points: 10

10

MEADOWSWEET

Scientific name
Filipendula ulmaria
When does it flower?
June–August
Where is it found?
Damp meadows, woods and ditches
What does it look like?
Tall, upright and leafy

ENCHANTER'S-NIGHTSHADE

Points: 20

20

Scientific name
Circaea lutetiana
When does it flower?
August–September
Where is it found?
Damp, shady woods
What does it look like?
Tall and single-stemmed with tiny flowers

COW PARSLEY

Points: 5 5

Scientific name
Anthriscus sylvestris
When does it flower?
May–June
Where is it found?
Woodland edges and
roadsides
What does it look like?
Up to 1 m (over 3 ft) tall with
branched flower heads
containing many flowers
arranged in an umbrella shape

10 **Points: 10**

WILD CARROT

Scientific name
Daucus carota
When does it flower?
June–September
Where is it found?
Chalky grasslands, especially
near the sea
What does it look like?
Similar to Cow Parsley
although the leaves are
different

5 Points: 5

HEDGE BINDWEED

Scientific name
Calystegia sepium
When does it flower?
June–August
Where is it found?
Hedges, woodland edges and gardens
What does it look like?
Twining plant with large, funnel-shaped flowers

RAMSONS

Points: 15

Scientific name
Allium ursinum
When does it flower?
April–June
Where is it found?
Damp woods and hedges
What does it look like?
Clusters of star-shaped flowers. The whole plant smells strongly of garlic so that it is often called Wild Garlic or Wood Garlic

11

DAISY

Points: 5 5

Scientific name
Bellis perennis
When does it flower?
Throughout the year
Where is it found?
Grassland including lawns
What does it look like?
A low plant with leaves arranged in a rosette

10 **Points: 10**

OXEYE DAISY

Scientific name
Leucanthemum vulgare
When does it flower?
May–September
Where is it found?
Most kinds of grassland
What does it look like?
Like a big daisy

GREATER PLANTAIN

Points: 5 5

Scientific name
Plantago major
When does it flower?
May–October
Where is it found?
Fields, gardens and waste ground
What does it look like?
A rosette of leaves from which the flower
spikes rise up to 50 cm (20 in.)

Points: 20

SUN SPURGE

Scientific name
Euphorbia helioscopa
When does it flower?
April–October
Where is it found?
Fields, gardens and waste
ground
What does it look like?
The 50 cm (20 in.) stem ends
in an umbrella-shaped flower
head

COMMON NETTLE

Points: 5
Double with answer 5

Scientific name
Urtica dioica
When does it flower?
June–September
Where is it found?
Woods, waste ground, hedgerows,
gardens
What does it look like?
Tall, hairy plant with roughly triangular,
saw-edged leaves

*The young leaves are good to eat – True
or False?*

13

WHITE DEAD-NETTLE

Points: 10

Scientific name
Lamium album
When does it flower?
May–August
Where is it found?
Roadsides, waste ground, hedgerows
What does it look like?
Similar to the Common Nettle but with large white flower heads and no stinging hairs

Points: 15
Double with answer

LORDS-AND-LADIES

Scientific name
Arum maculatum
When does it flower?
May–June
Where is it found?
Woodlands, hedgerows and ditches
What does it look like?
The flower spike is shrouded by a leafy cowl

What is the other well-known name for this plant?

Points: 10

Scientific name
Papaver rhoeas
When does it flower?
May–October
Where is it found?
Farmland and waste or
disturbed ground
What does it look like?
The tall stems are bristly while
the leaves are toothed

RED CAMPION

Points: 15

Scientific name
Silene dioica
When does it flower?
May–September
Where is it found?
Damp woods and hedgerows
What does it look like?
Similar to White Campion but
red and unscented

COMMON VALERIAN

Points: 20

Scientific name
Valeriana officinalis
When does it flower?
June–August
Where is it found?
Woods and roadsides
What does it look like?
Tall stems and tiny flowers in dense clusters

Points: 20

SCARLET PIMPERNEL

Scientific name
Anagallis arvensis
When does it flower?
May–October
Where is it found?
Cultivated ground, roadsides and sand dunes
What does it look like?
Small, ground-hugging plant

Also known as 'Poor Man's Weather Glass' because the flowers only open in the sunshine

Points: 15
Double with answer

BILBERRY

Scientific name
Vaccinium myrtillus
When does it flower?
April–June
Where is it found?
On heaths and moors and in woodlands on poor soils
What does it look like?
Thin woody stems with lots of bright green leaves

What colour are the edible fruits of the bilberry?

MUSK-MALLOW

Points: 25 Top Spot!

Scientific name
Malva moschata
When does it flower?
July–August
Where is it found?
Open, dry, grassy and bushy places, often on roadsides
What does it look like?
Hairy stems topped with clusters of big pink flowers

COMMON CENTAURY

Points: 20

Scientific name
Centaurium erythraea
When does it flower?
June–August
Where is it found?
All kinds of poor grassy places
What does it look like?
A basal rosette of pale green
leaves hugs the ground

Points: 10

RAGGED-ROBIN

Scientific name
Lychnis flos-cuculi
When does it flower?
May–August
Where is it found?
Damp meadows and woods
What does it look like?
As its name suggests, the
pink/red flowers have a
ragged appearance

Points: 25   Top Spot!

HERB-ROBERT

Scientific name
Geranium robertianum
When does it flower?
April–October
Where is it found?
Woods, hedgebanks, shingle
shores and mountains
What does it look like?
About 40 cm (16 in.) high with
hairy leaves and stalks

DOG-ROSE

Points: 10
Double with answer

Scientific name
Rosa canina
When does it flower?
June–July
Where is it found?
Woods, hedges and scrubland
What does it look like?
The bushes bear flowers that
are white or tinged with pink

What are the fruits called?

19

HEMP AGRIMONY

Points: 20

Scientific name
Eupatorium cannabinum
When does it flower?
July–September
Where is it found?
In damp woods and on marshy roadsides
What does it look like?
Masses of tall stems topped by dense pink flower heads

Points: 20

CROSS-LEAVED HEATH

Scientific name
Erica tetralix
When does it flower?
June–August
Where is it found?
In boggy heaths and moors
What does it look like?
Straggly, branching shrub with many small leaves measuring 2–4 mm (0.1–0.15 in.)

Points: 20

THRIFT

Scientific name
Armeria maritima
When does it flower?
April–August
Where is it found?
Sea cliffs and salt marshes
What does it look like?
Groups of plants form mat-like clumps and the pink flowers are sweet smelling

REDSHANK

Points: 15

Scientific name
Persicaria maculosa
When does it flower?
June–August
Where is it found?
Roadsides, ditches, waste ground and cornfields
What does it look like?
Has reddish stems and usually a dark blotch on each leaf

COMMON RESTHARROW

Points: 10

Scientific name
Ononis repens
When does it flower?
July–September
Where is it found?
In dry, grassy places
What does it look like?
Has a low, woody stem and small, downy leaves

Points: 10

CREEPING THISTLE

Scientific name
Cirsium arvense
When does it flower?
June–August
Where is it found?
Fields, roadsides and waste ground
What does it look like?
Masses of prickly stems and leaves

Points: 25 Top Spot!

BEE ORCHID

Scientific name
Ophrys apifera
When does it flower?
June–July
Where is it found?
Mainly on chalk and limestone downland
What does it look like?
Like a big furry bumble bee visiting a pink flower

BRAMBLE

Points: 10
Double with answer

Scientific name
Rubus fruticosus
When does it flower?
June–August
Where is it found?
Woods, roadsides, bushy places
What does it look like?
Has very prickly, arching stems and pink or white flowers

What is the fruit of the bramble called?

23

PINK TO RED FLOWERS

RED VALERIAN

Points: 25 Top Spot!

Scientific name
Centranthus ruber
When does it flower?
May–August
Where is it found?
Cliffs, quarries, walls and dry banks
What does it look like?
Grows in large tufts and has smooth, oval leaves and red, pink or white flowers

 **Points: 5**

FIELD BINDWEED

Scientific name
Convolvulus arvensis
When does it flower?
May–October
Where is it found?
Farms, gardens, roadsides and by railways
What does it look like?
A trailing or climbing plant with funnel-shaped pinkish, reddish or even white flowers

Points: 25 Top Spot!

Scientific name
Pedicularius sylvatica
When does it flower?
April–July
Where is it found?
Bogs, damp woods, moors and heaths where the soil is acid
What does it look like?
Quite variable in height with double-lipped flowers

CUCKOOFLOWER

Points: 15
Double with answer

Scientific name
Cardamine pratensis
When does it flower?
April–June
Where is it found?
Damp meadows, stream sides, ditches, roadsides and mountains
What does it look like?
Flower head contains between 7 and 20 four-petalled flowers varying from white to pink

What is this plant's other common name?

COMMON MALLOW

Points: 10 10

Scientific name
Malva sylvestris
When does it flower?
May–October
Where is it found?
Roadsides, meadows,
woodland
What does it look like?
The plant can reach heights of
1.5 m (5 ft)

15 **Points: 15**

RED CLOVER

Scientific name
Trifolium pratense
When does it flower?
May–October
Where is it found?
Grassland
What does it look like?
It may be upright or sprawling
with three-leaved stems

*This is grown as fodder for
cows and chickens*

Points: 20

SELFHEAL

Scientific name
Prunella vulgaris
When does it flower?
June–August
Where is it found?
In grassy places and in open woods
What does it look like?
Oval, pointed leaves on fairly short stems

This has been used in medicine for hundreds of years

TUFTED VETCH

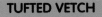

Points: 20

Scientific name
Vicia cracca
When does it flower?
June–August
Where is it found?
Roadside hedges, field and woodland edges
What does it look like?
A showy, pea-like plant which climbs using its tendrils

COMMON VETCH

Points: 20

Scientific name
Vicia sativa
When does it flower?
April–September
Where is it found?
Hedgerows, woodland and field edges
What does it look like?
A pea-like trailing or climbing plant with down-covered stems

 Points: 20

PURPLE-LOOSESTRIFE

Scientific name
Lythrum salicaria
When does it flower?
June–September
Where is it found?
Damp areas such as lakesides, stream sides or fens
What does it look like?
Strong-growing spikes up to 1.5 m (5 ft) tall

Points: 5
Double with answer

ROSEBAY WILLOWHERB

Scientific name
Chamerion angustifolium
When does it flower?
June–September
Where is it found?
Waste ground, rubbish tips, disturbed ground, cleared woodland
What does it look like?
Strong growing spikes up to 1.5 m (5 ft)

This plant is also called Fireweed; do you know why?

GREAT WILLOWHERB

Points: 10

Scientific name
Epilobium hirsutum
When does it flower?
July–September
Where is it found?
Woodlands, stream banks, ditches and marshes
What does it look like?
Bigger than Rosebay and with larger flowers at the top of the stem

HEATHER

Points: 10
Double with answer

Scientific name
Calluna vulgaris
When does it flower?
July–October
Where is it found?
Heaths, moors, open woods and boggy
areas on acid soil
What does it look like?
A bushy, shrub-like plant with spikes of
small flowers

It is also called Sling. True or False?

 Points: 15

BELL HEATHER

Scientific name
Erica cinerea
When does it flower?
May–September
Where is it found?
On the drier soils of acid heaths and
moors
What does it look like?
The flowers are larger and more bell-
shaped than those of Heather

Points: 15

BITTERSWEET

Scientific name
Solanum dulcamara
When does it flower?
May–September
Where is it found?
Damp hedges, woodlands and riverbanks
What does it look like?
It is a weak-growing, straggly plant which uses others for support

FOXGLOVE

Points: 10
Double with answer

10

Scientific name
Digitalis purpurea
When does it flower?
May–September
Where is it found?
Open woods, scrubland and hillsides on acid soils
What does it look like?
Tall, handsome spikes of thimble-shaped flowers

What organ of the human body is Digitalis used to treat?

STINKING IRIS

Points: 15

Scientific name
Iris foetidissima
When does it flower?
June
Where is it found?
In woods and scrub and on sea cliffs
What does it look like?
Thick tufts of evergreen leaves and bright orange seeds

Some people find the smell of the crushed leaves really unpleasant

 Points: 15

GROUND-IVY

Scientific name
Glechoma hederacea
When does it flower?
March–June
Where is it found?
Damp woods, hedges and waste ground
What does it look like?
This ground trailing plant has kidney-shaped leaves and it forms carpets where it grows. The leaves smell strongly when crushed

Points: 15

COMMON DOG-VIOLET

Scientific name
Viola riviniana
When does it flower?
April–June
Where is it found?
Woods, roadside banks and grassy fields
What does it look like?
A low-growing plant with heart-shaped leaves

RED DEAD-NETTLE

Points: 10

Scientific name
Lamium purpureum
When does it flower?
March–November
Where is it found?
Wasteland and cultivated ground
What does it look like?
Similar to other dead-nettles but with small,
reddish-purple flowers

Points: 15

LESSER BURDOCK

Scientific name
Arctium minus
When does it flower?
July–September
Where is it found?
Open woods, hedges and waste ground
What does it look like?
A tall, bushy plant with heart-shaped leaves

WATER MINT

Points: 15

Scientific name
Mentha aquatica
When does it flower?
July–September
Where is it found?
Bogs, marshes, lake and
stream sides
What does it look like?
Upright plant up to 80 cm
(32 in.) tall, smelling strongly
of mint

 Points: 15

SPEAR THISTLE

Scientific name
Cirsium vulgare
When does it flower?
July–September
Where is it found?
Grassy places, by roads,
waste ground
What does it look like?
Strong-growing plant with
prickly, winged stems and
spear-shaped leaf prickles

25 Points: 25 **Top Spot!**

GREEN ALKANET

Scientific name
Pentaglottis sempervirens
When does it flower?
April–August
Where is it found?
On roadsides near gardens
What does it look like?
Tall, rough stems with oval
leaves

VIPER'S-BUGLOSS

Points: 15 **15**

Scientific name
Echium vulgare
When does it flower?
May–September
Where is it found?
Chalk downs, shingles, dunes
What does it look like?
Tall, hairy plant with masses of
trumpet-shaped flowers

*This was once used as an
antivenin for snake bites*

HEDGE WOUNDWORT

Points: 15
Double with answer

Scientific name
Stachys sylvatica
When does it flower?
June–October
Where is it found?
Shady places such as woods and
hedgebanks
What does it look like?
Similar to a dead-nettle, with broad
leaves

How does this plant get its name?

Points: 20

MARSH WOUNDWORT

Scientific name
Stachys palustris
When does it flower?
July–August
Where is it found?
In marshy places and on damp
roadsides
What does it look like?
Similar to Hedge Woundwort but with
much narrower leaves and brighter
flowers

Points: 25   Top Spot!

MUSK THISTLE

Scientific name
Carduus nutans
When does it flower?
June–August
Where is it found?
In grassy and bushy places
What does it look like?
Has spiny stems and big, drooping flower-heads

BETONY

Points: 20

Scientific name
Stachys officinalis
When does it flower?
June–August
Where is it found?
In open grassy and bushy places
What does it look like?
Has slightly hairy, oblong leaves

PYRAMIDAL ORCHID

Points: 25 Top Spot! 25

Scientific name
Anacamptis pyramidalis
When does it flower?
July–August
Where is it found?
In chalk grassland and on
sand dunes
What does it look like?
The thin stems are topped
by a dome-shaped mass of
flowers

25 **Points: 25** Top Spot!

SOUTHERN MARSH-ORCHID

Scientific name
Dactylorhiza praetermissa
When does it flower?
June–July
Where is it found?
In open marshy places
What does it look like?
Has a stout stem and bright green
shiny leaves, sometimes spotted

Points: 20

WILD THYME

Scientific name
Thymus polytrichus
When does it flower?
April–September
Where is it found?
Dry grassland, heaths, dunes
What does it look like?
Ground-hugging plant which smells of the herb when crushed

WILD TEASEL

Points: 15

Scientific name
Dipsacus fullonum
When does it flower?
July–August
Where is it found?
Waste ground, open woods, riverbanks
What does it look like?
Strongly growing, large plant with prickly flower heads

BLACK HOREHOUND

Points: 20 20

Scientific name
Ballota nigra
When does it flower?
June–August
Where is it found?
In hedgebanks and bushy places, often near houses
What does it look like?
A bushy, weedy plant with a strong, unpleasant smell

25 **Points: 25** **Top Spot!**

EARLY PURPLE ORCHID

Scientific name
Orchis mascula
When does it flower?
April–June
Where is it found?
Chalky woods, downs and sea cliffs
What does it look like?
A typical orchid with the rosette of leaves spotted in a purplish colour

Points: 15
Double with answer

MEADOW CRANE'S-BILL

Scientific name
Geranium pratense
When does it flower?
May–August
Where is it found?
Roadsides, hedgerows, edges of grassy meadows
What does it look like?
Strongly growing plant with deeply divided leaves

How does the plant get its name?

SHEEP'S-BIT

Points: 25 Top Spot!

Scientific name
Jasione montana
When does it flower?
May–July
Where is it found?
On acid soils, on heaths, moors, grassy roadsides, cliffs and shingle
What does it look like?
Fairly low, wiry stems topped with blue 'pom-pom' flower heads

GERMANDER SPEEDWELL

Points: 15

Scientific name
Veronica chamaedrys
When does it flower?
April–July
Where is it found?
Grassland, hedges, roadsides, open woodland
What does it look like?
The stems grow along the ground at first before reaching upwards

 Points: 15

HEATH SPEEDWELL

Scientific name
Veronica officinalis
When does it flower?
May–August
Where is it found?
On grassy heaths and moors
What does it look like?
Creeping, hairy stems and leaves with erect flower spikes

Points: 15

BUGLE

Scientific name
Ajuga reptans
When does it flower?
May–June
Where is it found?
Damp grassland and woodland
clearings
What does it look like?
The stems are hairy on two
opposite sides and the flowers
appear in rings around the stem

HAREBELL

Points: 15

Scientific name
Campanula rotundifolia
When does it flower?
August–September
Where is it found?
Dry, chalky grassland
What does it look like?
Nodding thin stalks, thin leaves
and bell-shaped flowers

43

CHICORY

Points: 15
Double with answer

Scientific name
Cichorium intybus
When does it flower?
June–September
Where is it found?
Roadsides, grassy places and waste ground
What does it look like?
A rather straggling and stiff-stemmed plant

If roasted and powdered, the roots are used as a substitute for coffee. True or False?

10 **Points: 10**

BLUEBELL

Scientific name
Hyacinthoides non-scripta
When does it flower?
April–June
Where is it found?
Woodlands and other shady, damp places
What does it look like?
The leaves are narrow and shiny and surround the flower stem

Points: 10

10

COMMON KNAPWEED

Scientific name
Centaurea nigra
When does it flower?
June–August
Where is it found?
In all kinds of grassy places
What does it look like?
Stiff, upright stems with uncut leaves

Bees and other insects love this plant for its nectar

GREATER KNAPWEED

Points: 15

15

Scientific name
Centaurea scabiosa
When does it flower?
June–September
Where is it found?
Dry grassland, hedgebanks, roadsides
What does it look like?
Stiff, branched stems with deeply cut leaves

MARSH-MARIGOLD

Points: 10 (10)

Scientific name
Caltha palustris
When does it flower?
March–May
Where is it found?
Marshes, ditches and the edges of watercourses
What does it look like?
Like a large buttercup with round leaves

(5) **Points: 5**

CREEPING BUTTERCUP

Scientific name
Ranunculus repens
When does it flower?
April–September
Where is it found?
Damp meadows and roadsides
What does it look like?
The plant is tough, tall, hairy and has palm-like leaves

Points: 15

YELLOW WATER-LILY

Scientific name
Nuphar lutea
When does it flower?
June–September
Where is it found?
In lakes, ponds and slow-running streams
What does it look like?
The roundish leathery leaves float at the surface and the flowers are carried above them

WILD MIGNONETTE

Points: 15

Scientific name
Reseda lutea
When does it flower?
June–September
Where is it found?
Disturbed ground and wasteland
What does it look like?
The bristly stems carry spikes of pale yellow flowers

The name comes from the French for 'dainty'

PERFORATE ST JOHN'S-WORT

Points: 15

Scientific name
Hypericum perforatum
When does it flower?
May–September
Where is it found?
Open woods, scrub, dry
grassland
What does it look like?
When held up to the light the
leaves seem to be marked
with pale spots

Points: 15

COMMON ROCK-ROSE

Scientific name
Helianthemum nummularium
When does it flower?
May–September
Where is it found?
Dry chalk grasslands
What does it look like?
The flower looks like a single
yellow rose

Points: 15

KIDNEY VETCH

Scientific name
Anthyllis vulneraria
When does it flower?
April–September
Where is it found?
Dry grassland, dunes, sea cliffs
What does it look like?
The flowers are carried in round
clusters at the top of the stem

AGRIMONY

Points: 15

Scientific name
Agrimonia eupatoria
When does it flower?
June–September
Where is it found?
Dry fields, roadsides, wasteland
What does it look like?
Upright, sometimes reddish
stems with saw-edged leaflets

SILVERWEED

Points: 15
Double with answer

Scientific name
Potentilla anserina
When does it flower?
May–September
Where is it found?
Damp fields, hedgebanks,
roadsides, wasteland
What does it look like?
The leaves are arranged in
rosettes from which runners
creep

How did this get its name?

Points: 20

CREEPING CINQUEFOIL

Scientific name
Potentilla reptans
When does it flower?
May–September
Where is it found?
Dry roadsides and wasteland
What does it look like?
A creeping, mat-forming plant
with long runners

*The name comes from the
Latin for 'five leaves'*

Points: 15

COWSLIP

Scientific name
Primula veris
When does it flower?
April–May
Where is it found?
Hedgebanks, roadsides, old meadows
What does it look like?
The rosette of Primrose-like leaves surround a medium-height flower stem

PRIMROSE

Points: 10
Double for finding both kinds

Scientific name
Primula vulgaris
When does it flower?
March–May
Where is it found?
Woods and banks beside roads and railways
What does it look like?
The flowers may be either pin-eyed (long style) or thrum-eyed (short style)

The plant in the picture is pin-eyed

51

YELLOW PIMPERNEL

Points: 25 Top Spot! 25

Scientific name
Lysimachia nemorum
When does it flower?
May–July
Where is it found?
In dampish woods
What does it look like?
Creeping stems in large
masses

10 **Points: 10**

COMMON TOADFLAX

Scientific name
Linaria vulgaris
When does it flower?
July–September
Where is it found?
Grassy places and waste ground
What does it look like?
Like a small-flowered garden
snapdragon

Points: 25 Top Spot!

CORN MARIGOLD

Scientific name
Chrysanthemum segetum
When does it flower?
May–August
Where is it found?
In arable fields with wheat or other crops
What does it look like?
Masses of bright yellow flowers on tall stems

BULRUSH

Points: 5

Scientific name
Typha latifolia
When does it flower?
June–August
Where is it found?
Edges of rivers, lakes and ponds
What does it look like?
Long, stiff grey leaves and sausage shaped flower spikes

The roots provide a safe place for young fish to hide

53

LESSER CELANDINE

Points: 15

Scientific name
Ranunculus ficaria
When does it flower?
March–May
Where is it found?
Hedgerows, gardens, roadsides and woods
What does it look like?
A low-growing buttercup with heart-shaped leaves

Points: 15

GREAT MULLEIN

Scientific name
Verbascum thapsus
When does it flower?
June–August
Where is it found?
Dry, grassy or stony places
What does it look like?
It may reach 2 m (over 6 ft) in height; the leaves and stem are woolly

Points: 10

HONEYSUCKLE

Scientific name
Lonicera periclymenum
When does it flower?
June–October
Where is it found?
Woodlands and hedgerows
What does it look like?
A woody climbing plant with
sweet-smelling flowers

SMOOTH HAWK'S-BEARD

Points: 10

Scientific name
Crepis capillaris
When does it flower?
June–November
Where is it found?
Grassland and waste ground
What does it look like?
The flowers resemble small
Dandelions carried on tall, thin
stems

COMMON RAGWORT

Points: 5

Scientific name
Senecio jacobaea
When does it flower?
May–October
Where is it found?
Neglected fields, dunes and
roadsides
What does it look like?
An upright, branched plant
with strong-smelling leaves
that are poisonous to livestock

Points: 20

TRAVELLER'S-JOY

Scientific name
Clematis vitalba
When does it flower?
July–September
Where is it found?
In woods and hedgerows,
mainly on chalk and limestone
What does it look like?
A big, woody climber with
fragrant flowers

Points: 15

GOLDENROD

Scientific name
Solidago virgaurea
When does it flower?
July–October
Where is it found?
Dry woods, hedges, dunes, grassy
and rocky places
What does it look like?
The flowerhead takes the form of
a branched spike with many tiny
flowers

DANDELION

Points: 5
Double with answer

Scientific name
Taraxacum officinale
When does it flower?
Irregularly throughout the year
Where is it found?
Road verges, gardens,
farmland, waste ground, fields
What does it look like?
The flower stems are hollow
and contain a milky juice

*Where does the name come
from?*

PERENNIAL SOW-THISTLE

Points: 10 10

Scientific name
Sonchus arvensis
When does it flower?
August–September
Where is it found?
Gardens, farms, roadsides,
waste ground
What does it look like?
Similar to the Dandelion, but
with many flowers on each
stalk rather than a single
flower

25 **Points: 25   Top Spot!**

CARLINE THISTLE

Scientific name
Carlina vulgaris
When does it flower?
July–August
Where is it found?
Dry grassland
What does it look like?
Low-growing and prickly

Points: 25 **Top Spot!**

GOLDEN SAMPHIRE

Scientific name
Inula crithmoides
When does it flower?
July–August
Where is it found?
On sea cliffs and salt marshes
What does it look like?
A big, fleshy-leaved daisy

COMMON FLEABANE

Points: 20

Scientific name
Pulicaria dysenterica
When does it flower?
July–September
Where is it found?
Ditches, marshy meadows and
damp roadsides
What does it look like?
A big, shaggy plant with masses
of yellow flowers

LADY'S BEDSTRAW

Points: 20

Scientific name
Galium verum
When does it flower?
July–August
Where is it found?
In dry, grassy places
What does it look like?
Masses of tiny, yellow flowers on sprawling stems

The name comes from the fact that people used to use this plant for bedding!

Points: 20

WOOD SAGE

Scientific name
Teucrium scorodonia
When does it flower?
July–September
Where is it found?
Woodland edges, hedgebanks and other fairly dry places
What does it look like?
A downy plant about 30 cm (1ft) high with wrinkled leaves

Points: 15

COLT'S-FOOT

Scientific name
Tussilago farfara
When does it flower?
February–April
Where is it found?
Wasteland, dunes, riversides
What does it look like?
Dandelion-like flower but the
leaves are heart-shaped

YELLOW IRIS

Points: 10

Scientific name
Iris pseudacorus
When does it flower?
May–August
Where is it found?
Ditches, lakesides, riversides,
wet woods
What does it look like?
Like a yellow garden iris

BROOM

Points: 5

Scientific name
Cytisus scoparius
When does it flower?
May–June
Where is it found?
On dry, acid soils such as heaths
What does it look like?
A small, dark green, spineless shrub

Points: 5

GORSE

Scientific name
Ulex europaeus
When does it flower?
March–June
Where is it found?
Heaths and hillsides
What does it look like?
A spiky bush

Some people think the flowers smell of coconut

INDEX

Answers: P6 Jack-by-the-hedge, Jack-among-the-hedgerow **P13:** True (but they should never be eaten raw) **P14:** Cuckoo pint **P17:** Black **P19:** Hips **P23:** Blackberry **P25:** Lady's smock **P29:** Because it grows on burnt ground **P30:** False. It is called Ling **P31:** The heart **P36:** Because the leaves were once used to dress wounds **P41:** From the beak of the fruit, which resembles a Crane's bill **P44:** True **P50:** Because the silky hairs make the underside of the leaves look silvery **P58:** Dent de lion (French for 'lion's tooth'), which refers to the toothed leaves

i-SPY

How to get your
i-SPY certificate
and badge

Let us know when you've become
a super-spotter with 1000 points
and we'll send you a special
certificate and badge!

HERE'S
WHAT
TO DO!

- ✓ Ask an adult to check your score.

- ✓ Visit www.collins.co.uk/i-SPY to
  apply for your certificate. If you
  are under the age of 13 you will need
  a parent or guardian to do this.

- ✓ We'll send your certificate via
  email and you'll receive a brilliant
  badge through the post!

DAILY LIFE
in
Ancient Greece

by Lisa M. Bolt Simons

Raintree is an imprint of Capstone Global Library Limited, a company incorporated in England and Wales having its registered office at 264 Banbury Road, Oxford, OX2 7DY – Registered company number: 6695582

www.raintree.co.uk
myorders@raintree.co.uk

Edited by Aaron Sautter
Designed by Bobbie Nuytten
Picture research by Svetlana Zhurkin
Production by Jennifer Walker

ISBN 978 1 4747 1744 1 (hardback)
19 18 17 16 15
10 9 8 7 6 5 4 3 2 1

ISBN 978 1 4747 1748 9 (paperback)
20 19 18 17 16
10 9 8 7 6 5 4 3 2 1

British Library Cataloguing in Publication Data
A full catalogue record for this book is available from the British Library.

Photo Credits
Alamy: Mary Evans Picture Library, 13, North Wind Picture Archives, 9, 11, 19, 21; National Geographic Creative: H.M. Herget, cover (top), 7, 15; Newscom: Universal Images Group/Leemage, 14; Shutterstock: Arkady Chubykin, cover (bottom), 1, Dhoxax, 8, Emi Cristea, 18, Ensuper (paper), back cover and throughout, ilolab (grunge background), cover, 1, James Steidl, 20, Kamira, back cover (bottom right), Madlen, 12, Maxim Kostenko (background), 2 and throughout, mexrix, 5 (back), Roberto Castillo (column), back cover and throughout; Wikipedia: MatthiasKabel/Sting, 17;
XNR Productions, 5 (map)

We would like to thank Jonathan M. Hall, professor at the University of Chicago, for his invaluable help in the preparation of this book.

Every effort has been made to contact copyright holders of material reproduced in this book. Any omissions will be rectified in subsequent printings if notice is given to the publisher.

All the internet addresses (URLs) given in this book were valid at the time of going to press. However, due to the dynamic nature of the internet, some addresses may have changed, or sites may have changed or ceased to exist since publication. While the author and publisher regret any inconvenience this may cause readers, no responsibility for any such changes can be accepted by either the author or the publisher.

Printed and bound in China.

CONTENTS

GROWING UP
IN ANCIENT GREECE

Imagine growing up in Greece 3,000 years ago. You wake up on a mattress filled with grass or feathers. If you're a boy, you may go to school. If you're a girl, a **tutor** teaches you at home instead. During free time you can play with your toys. These include clay figures, wax dolls or balls made from pig bladders. Welcome to life in ancient Greece!

FACT:
Students often did schoolwork on a wooden tablet that was filled with wax. They wrote on the wax with a bone or metal **stylus**. The wax could be smoothed out to erase the work and continue writing.

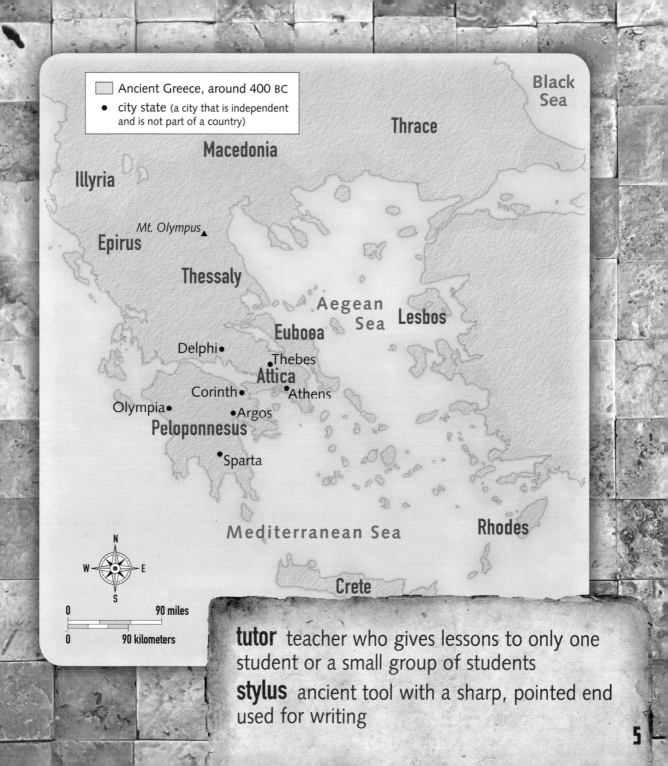

Ancient Greece, around 400 BC

• city state (a city that is independent and is not part of a country)

Black Sea

Thrace

Macedonia

Illyria

Mt. Olympus ▲

Epirus

Thessaly

Aegean Sea

Lesbos

Euboea

Delphi •

• Thebes

Attica

Corinth •

• Athens

Olympia •

• Argos

Peloponnesus

• Sparta

Mediterranean Sea

Rhodes

N
W   E
S

0   90 miles

0   90 kilometers

Crete

tutor teacher who gives lessons to only one student or a small group of students

stylus ancient tool with a sharp, pointed end used for writing

5

Whether rich or poor, people's lives were busy in ancient Greece. Children in **wealthy** families were usually sent to school or taught at home. But poor families usually made children do chores at home instead. Men fought in the army or had jobs outside the home. Most women stayed at home to run their houses or manage the family's **slaves**.

A FATHER'S DECISION

Greek fathers could choose to accept or reject a newborn baby. If he named the baby within 10 days of its birth, it became part of the family. But if he rejected the baby, it was often placed in a clay pot and left by the road. A different family could then adopt the baby.

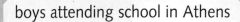
boys attending school in Athens

wealthy having a great deal of money
slave person who is owned by
another person and is forced to work
without pay

LIFE AT HOME

Clothing

Most families in ancient Greece made their own clothes. Everyone wore free-flowing clothes called **tunics**. Cloaks were also worn in cold weather. At first, nearly everybody's clothes were white. But people began to wear brightly coloured clothing around 500 BC. Some people wore strapped sandals or boots to protect their feet, but many went barefoot.

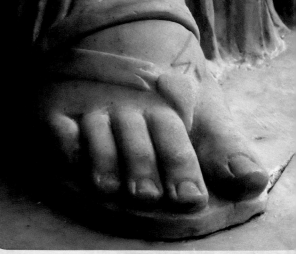

tunic loose, sleeveless garment

The ancient Greeks often wore colourful, loose-fitting clothing.

Houses

Ancient Greek houses were made of wood, mud bricks or stone. Two or three rooms were built around a **courtyard**. Men, women and children had separate rooms. Every house had an altar for making animal **sacrifices** to the gods. Most houses didn't have a bathroom. Instead, people used **chamber pots** or went outside.

courtyard open area surrounded by walls
sacrifice offering made to a god
chamber pot type of bowl that people used as a toilet

FACT:
 Wealthy women rarely left the house. If they did go outside, they always went with a slave or male companion. Poor women were allowed outside, but only to work. They went alone to fetch water, shop for food or help their husbands with farm work.

Food

The ancient Greeks ate three meals a day. Fish and seafood were popular. People also ate a lot of bread, fruit, garlic and onions. Much of the food was cooked in olive oil. People ate their food with their fingers. They usually drank water or wine mixed with water.

THE IMPORTANT OLIVE TREE

Olive trees were very important to the ancient Greeks. Greeks often ate olives. They used olive oil for cooking, lighting lamps and making skin care products. Olive oil was also sold to other countries. Olympic winners' crowns were even made of olive tree leaves woven together.

The ancient Greeks sometimes ate their meals while lying on couches.

13

EDUCATION AND WORK

Work

Greek men were expected to work outside the home. Many served in the military. Others worked as fishermen, farmers, **craftsmen** or artists. Farmers grew crops, such as barley and wheat, in fields close to home. Craftsmen worked in shops around the **agora**.

This vase painting shows how Greeks gathered olives.

craftsmen people who are skilled at making things with their hands

agora open marketplace in ancient Greece

Military education in Sparta

Most young Greek men went to military school at the age of 18. They trained to be soldiers or sailors in the navy. They prepared for the battles that often happened between Greek **city states**.

Military training was especially tough in the city state of Sparta. Boys were sent to live at military schools at age the age of seven. They trained very hard and had little food or clothing, no shoes and hard beds. Young men took a fitness test between the ages of 18 and 20. If a man didn't pass, he was no longer considered a citizen of Sparta.

city state city that is independent and is not part of a country

large, square sails to provide speed on open sea

FACT:
The Greek navy had many large ships called triremes. They were about 37 metres (120 feet) long. A trireme needed 170 men to row the ship's oars.

37 metres (120 feet) long

200 crew members, including rowers

Ancient Greek trireme

170 oars on three levels

RELIGION AND THE ARTS

Honouring the gods

Religion was a big part of ancient Greek life. The Greeks believed in many gods. Many large temples were built for the gods. Each temple honoured a certain god and included a statue of the god inside. The Greeks often performed animal sacrifices and held other **ceremonies** to please their gods.

ceremony special actions, words or music performed to mark an important event

temple to the Greek god, Hephaestus

statue of the Greek goddess, Athena

19

Arts and entertainment

The ancient Greeks enjoyed several forms of entertainment. They danced, sang and played instruments, such as **lyres**. The Greeks built large, open-air theatres into hillsides. They performed plays in the theatres to honour the gods. Singers and poets also told tales of Greek heroes and gods for audiences at the theatres.

lyre small, stringed, harplike instrument

a theatre in ancient Athens

21

Glossary

agora open marketplace in ancient Greece

ceremony special actions, words or music performed to mark an important event

chamber pot type of bowl that people used as a toilet

city state city that is independent and is not part of a country

courtyard open area surrounded by walls

craftsmen people who are skilled at making things with their hands

lyre small, stringed, harplike instrument

sacrifice offering made to a god

slave person who is owned by another person and is forced to work without pay

stylus ancient tool with a sharp pointed end used for writing

tunic loose, sleeveless garment

tutor teacher who gives lessons to only one student or a small group of students

wealthy having a great deal of money

Read more

Ancient Greeks (Beginners), Stephanie Turnball (Usborne Publishing Ltd, 2015)

Geography Matters in Ancient Greece (Geography Matters in Ancient Civilizations) Melanie Waldron (Heinemann Raintree, 2015)

You Wouldn't Want to be a Slave in Ancient Greece!: A Life You'd Rather Not Have (You Wouldn't Want To), Fiona Macdonald (Franklin Watts, 2014)

Websites

www.ancientgreece.co.uk
Learn all about ancient Greece on The British Museum website.

www.bbc.co.uk/history/anicent/greeks/
Explore topics about ancient Greeks, such as the Olympic Games, theatres and gods.

Comprehension questions

1. The ancient Greeks believed in many gods. Name three ways in which they honoured and worshiped the gods.

2. Why do you think boys in Sparta went to live at tough military schools at such a young age?

Index